Praise for *21 Ways to [Powerfully Network] Your Business* and Kristen Eckstein

"Do you really know *how* to network? Kristen Eckstein answers that question and more in her latest book, *21 Ways to Powerfully Network Your Business*. Not only do I use her easy-to-implement techniques, I recommend her to all of my clients."

—Linette Daniels, author of *Passion Won't Pay the Bills*
www.EmpowerMoreYouth.com

"*21 Ways to Powerfully Network Your Business* is the best 'little black book' of networking and wonderfully illustrates the importance of building solid relationships. Kristen shares no-nonsense techniques to prepare you for your next event. Pick up your copy today."

—Kelli Claypool, President & CEO Small Business and Learning Institute
www.BusinessAndLearning.com

"Imagine going into a room and knowing no one. How can you make an impact? How can you be heard? Kristen Eckstein's *21 Ways to Powerfully Network Your Business* is the answer. It will give you a variety of ways (21 to be exact!) to find your voice and create a powerful presence that brings you more visibility, credibility, and profits. A perfect gift for anyone attending a live event for sure!"

—Shannon Cherry, Your Creative Relationship Marketing Expert
www.BeHeardSolutions.com

"*21 Ways to Powerfully Network Your Business* by Kristen Eckstein is an easy-to-read book that is full of practical tips to take your business to the next level. It is a phenomenal way for new business owners to start their businesses off on the right foot, and it is also great for seasoned business owners to read to enhance their networking skills. Give this book to all the people you know who are working on establishing a solid plan for meeting customers to grow their businesses."

—Stevii Mills, Founder of *The Beauty From Head To Toe Tour*

"Kristen Eckstein shares the secrets of networking in her latest book—21 Ways to Powerfully Network Your Business. You no longer need to be afraid of how to approach people in the social scenes, how to dress, where to sit… Kristen shares all that information and more in this little book—definitely a must have in your library."

—Lisa Benavidez, Event Planner for MCE OnSite

"Kristen is such a joy to work with and honestly, one of the most efficient, action-oriented and conscientious providers I've ever worked with. She is one of my favorite resources to recommend!"

—Carrie Wilkerson, The Barefoot Executive™, BarefootExecutive.tv

"Kristen's heart for business-done-right and business-done-well are at the very core of here interactions, and it shows. She's a natural 'connector' and a true resource for all entrepreneurs. She's wonderfully unforgettable."

—Jenna Lang, Content Consultant

21 Ways to Powerfully Network Your Business

21 WAYS

to
powerfully
network
your
business

Kristen Eckstein

Discover BOOKS™
an Imprint of Imagine! Books™

High Point, North Carolina

21 Ways™ Series, Book 2

Published by Discover! Books™
an Imprint of Imagine! Books™
PO Box 16268, High Point, NC 27261
contact@artsimagine.com

Imagine! Books™ is an enterprise of Imagine! Studios™
Visit us online at www.artsimagine.com

Copyright © 2011 Kristen Eckstein
Cover Design © 2011 Imagine! Studios™
Illustrations by Drawperfect, purchased at istockphoto.com

All rights reserved. No part of this publication may be reproduced or transmitted in any form or by any means, including informational storage and retrieval systems, without permission in writing from the copyright holder, except for brief quotations in a review.

ISBN 13: 978-0-9767913-8-6
Library of Congress Control Number: 2011933263

First Discover! Books™ printing, July 2011

Dedication

To entrepreneurs everywhere who genuinely want to make a difference in the world.

You are *not* crazy.

Acknowledgements

Many thanks to:

My first mentor, Barbara Skivington, who taught me the value of putting others first in my business.

My coaches through the years: Mack Arrington, Carrie Wilkerson, Bob the Teacher Jenkins, Felicia Slattery, and Shannon Cherry. Learning from you is the secret to my success.

My editor, Erin Casey, for all your hard work making the text (and me) look great.

My husband and guru book designer, Joe Eckstein, for making the design of this book series stand out from the crowd. And for your support with this crazy idea we started called a business.

All my clients past, present, and future, with whom I have built solid relationships. Without you, I would not be in business, and I would be without the best of friends.

Introduction

Let's face it. Running a business is hard work. Still—even when we wake up and wonder how it came to this, how we got here, and why someone in their right mind is awake at four in the morning—we love our businesses.

Why? Because when we implement the great idea that woke us up before the crack of dawn, that idea then works for us. We know that those pesky, brilliant ideas combined with our passion for what we do generate income for us while we enjoy the luxury of taking a nap in the afternoon.

Few people will ever understand the passion entrepreneurs feel for what they do. Thus, the relationships we build around our businesses may lead to some of our deepest friendships. Relationships drive and continuously fuel our businesses. But building relationships takes time, hard work, and typically begins at a networking event or conference when we meet people for the first time.

I decided to write this book because so many people have asked me how they can easily make a bigger impact on their businesses through stronger relationships and networking, as I have. I hope you enjoy discovering what I have learned through the years. But more than that, I hope you will use these simple, powerful strategies to grow your business in a meaningful way.

Happy Networking!

WAY 1

Bring Plenty of Business Cards

When you attend local networking events or conferences, one of the biggest mistakes you can make is to not have any method of giving your contact information to other attendees. There *will* be people interested in doing business with you, so make sure you have plenty of business cards handy! Here are my five top tips for effective business cards:

Make them professional

If you have an arts-and-crafts business, it is perfectly acceptable to create your own business cards. Each card would be unique and represent your skill in an artistic, one-of-a-kind way. However, if you are in any other field get your card professionally designed and printed. You do not want your cards to scream, "I printed these at home because I'm cheap!" Nor do you want cards that look like everyone else's because you are all using the same generic template and the same cheap paper. Your cards are the second impression people receive when they first meet you (see "Way 16" for the first). Make them professional.

Use both sides

The back of your business card is powerful real estate, so don't waste it! If you typically write appointments on the back of your cards, make them look more professional with "Date: _____ Time: _____" spaces to be filled in. If you do not need appointment-style cards, use the back of your card to direct people to your website for a free gift (and to sign up on your email list).

Avoid using too many words

A good graphic designer will be able to place all your information in a way that is both professional and readable. But remember, your space is limited. Even if you opt for the more expensive bi-fold cards to double your workable space, you need to keep in mind that less is more. Use pictures wherever possible and condense your descriptive text to only feature the highlights of what you do. Using a smaller font so you can fit more information clutters the space and makes it completely unreadable.

Invest in a logo

A logo is more quickly recognizable than a photo of yourself. If you are an entrepreneur with your own business, make sure you have a logo that is eye catching and will look good printed on the small space of a business card. If you need help with your logo design, check out ArtsImagine.com. If you represent a direct selling company, you need to make sure you can use their logo and follow their guidelines in the design of your card. Some MLMs and direct selling companies only allow you to use their logo or name on cards they provide, so be sure to know what your organization's rules are.

Avoid cheap companies like Vistaprint

The reason I recommend avoiding companies like Vistaprint is that while they are good for a basic calling card or a temporary card, the cards they offer are usually printed on cheap paper and are hard to read. They have some nice templates, but with so many other people using the same templates, your card can easily get confused for someone else's—that is not good brand building. Your best option is to hire a professional graphic designer to help you format a personalized, readable card. Keep in mind if you go with a cheap card, it tells your potential customer *you* are cheap and may not do the most professional job for them. People look for quality, so be sure you reflect that in the materials you send home with them.

Think Bigger

In addition to typical business cards, think outside the box. For instance, if I were a business coach or professional speaker on networking for your business, I would use a book (like this one) as an oversized, very informative business card. The backmatter of your book can feature additional programs and services you offer, as well as other books or materials you've published. A book, unlike a brochure, business card or flier, is a business tool that isn't likely to end up in a garbage as soon as someone gets home from an event—especially if you take the time to autograph it for them!

You may also consider a unique gift that is branded with your business logo and contact information. Nowadays you can find everything from pens to portfolio bags to USB drives—all that can be customized with your information. The more useful the gift, the less likely your contact information will end up in the trash can, and the more likely it is to stay in front of your prospect for months to come. Check out UniqueMarketingTools.com for thousands of such items.

Think of a unique item that fits your business and style. Give your distinct "business card" as a free gift, and don't be afraid to pass them out.

If you would like to create a book as a business card, check out WriteMyBookIn3Days.com for a free video on how to get your book written fast.

WAY 2

Listen—*Really* Listen

I'm sure you've heard the saying, "You have two ears and only one mouth." The premise is we should listen twice as much as we speak. Next time you attend a networking event, look around. How many people are talking vs. listening? Who do you remember best? The person who rattled off their thirty-second elevator pitch to you and then launched into a fifteen-minute description of their business and how it can solve the problem they think you have? Or, do you remember the person who listened to you talk about your business (or anything else you chose to talk about)?

Most of those who attend networking events tend to be extraverts. I admit it, I'm a classic extravert. My weakness is talking nonstop and not giving anyone else time to speak. It takes great effort for me to force myself to shut up and listen—*really listen*—to the other person. But I can tell you one amazing thing: When I choose to listen, no matter what the other person is talking about, whether it's personal or business, when I listen even though I know I will never use their services, that person remembers *me*.

It is not important how many contacts you can give business cards to or how many people you can meet in one night. In fact, if you think networking equates to running around the room and shoving business cards into people's hands, do yourself a favor and save a tree—STOP. That careless behavior guarantees that most of your cards will end up in the trash. Once again, it isn't quantity that matters. What is important is the *quality* of the relationship you establish with the person you've just met. And forming a quality relationship begins with the simple act of listening.

Here are a few effective listening skills that will help you gain business from those who remember you:

Look them in the eye

Engage them with your eyes so they know you are paying attention. See "Way 3" for more information on eye contact.

Don't just nod your head

Repeat something important they say back to them. This will show them you really listened.

Do not finish their sentences

There are some people who will finish every sentence you say. That is annoying! This bad habit gives the impression that you are in a hurry and do not have time to fully listen to them.

It's OK if the other person talks so much that you never get a chance to tell them what you do. Simply ask them for their card and hand them yours in return before leaving the conversation. I guarantee they will remember you and your business because you *listened*.

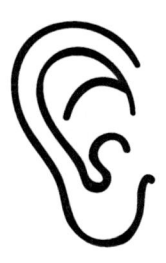

WAY 3

Make Solid Eye Contact

When networking, making *solid* eye contact while in a conversation with someone is absolutely crucial. When greeting someone, look them in the eye. As you listen to them, maintain eye contact. If you let your gaze wander, it tells the other person they are unimportant or uninteresting. Your lack of attention is a signal that you want to move on to someone else. Regardless of who you are speaking with, make eye contact with them during the entire conversation.

Think about how important and valued you've felt in the past when someone maintained eye contact with you throughout your conversation with them. Your desire should be to make others feel the same way. People do not want to do business with a company or idea. They want to know they are cared about, and they want to know *you*. Eye contact builds trust, integrity, and even friendship.

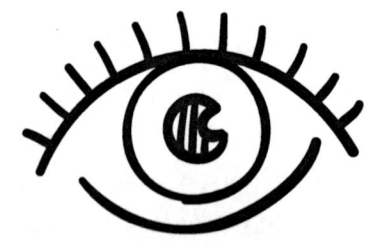

WAY 4

Shake with a Firm Hand

When you attend a networking event you will shake dozens of hands. Some handshakes leave you feeling confident that the other person may be able to serve your needs, and other handshakes make you want to run away and wash your hands a dozen times. Here are a few different types of handshakes I have identified during my own networking experiences:

The dead fish

Have you ever shaken hands with someone whose hand felt limp in yours? Their lack of engagement may have made you feel like you were crushing their hand. Or, their limpness makes you feel like you should be kissing the hand of royalty.

I call this the "dead fish." If you offer a "dead fish" (yuck!) to someone, they will immediately perceive you as weak and unconfident. Don't do it.

The two-hander

Some people shake with both hands. They grab you with a nice firm handshake, then their other hand closes in on top of yours so they are completely surrounding you. It may make you feel powerless or as if they are trying to take control of you.

Remember, your introductory handshake is usually given to someone who doesn't know you or your personality. Allow them some control in deciding when to let go. The two-hander takes control from the other person and instantly puts them on the defensive. Do not be a two-hander hand shaker.

The confident networker

The confident networker is easy to spot. They walk around the room straight and tall, they smile and look others in the eye. And when they walk up to you, they extend one hand and offer a nice, firm, but not overbearing grip. They exude confidence and give the other person a sense of importance and control.

This is the person you should aspire to be. Even if you feel like a dead fish or if you are a Type A who is accustomed to being in charge, the confident networker is ultimately the one who will give the best first impression.

WAY 5

Carry Hand Sanitizer

Most networking events feature a lot of hand shaking. A *lot*. And, most events provide finger foods. All those hands reach for the food before, during, and after touching dozens of other hands. There is bound to be someone at every event who came sick, is just getting over being sick, or who is starting to get sick. It is like school—rooms filled with germs and people spreading them.

A couple of years ago I received one of the best gifts anyone could give—a small bottle of hand sanitizer housed in a rubber holder that straps to anything. I cannot tell you how many of those little bottles I have gone through since!

I have hand sanitizer in colors to match my brand (check out Bath and Body Works) attached to my handbag, laptop bag, and carry-on suitcase. I also keep one in the glove compartment of my car. My frequent illnesses have decreased, and when people see me using it they instantly want some, too.

At a recent conference, one of the guest speakers had us do an exercise. We were to run around the room and shake hands with as many people as we could in three minutes. I honestly do not remember the point of the exercise. It was fun, I got to say hello to people I had not met, and after the exercise I whipped out my vanilla-scented hand sanitizer and cleansed my hands. Then I got an idea and offered a little to the people around me. Then I decided to travel around the room before everyone sat back down and gave it to as many people as possible. People were grateful I had thought of their health. That simple act let them know I really cared about them as people, not just another business contact.

Get a miniature bottle of hand sanitizer and carry it with you. You never know when that little bottle will make you a hero!

WAY 6

Smile!

There are two ways to break any language barrier in the world: music and a smile. Both invoke an emotion, but only a smile shows personal attention and makes the other person feel important and special. When attending networking events, make sure you bring your most valuable asset: your smile. Your smile not only makes you look younger, brighter, and more engaging, but it immediately puts others at ease.

How many times have you been to an event where you knew no one? I can be uncomfortable to approach others for the first time. Even as an extravert I struggle with those unsettling feelings on a regular basis. But, if someone approaches me wearing a genuine smile, I am instantly put at ease. This is the reaction you want from others. You want them to feel comfortable, welcomed, and liked. When they know you like them, it is easier for them to like you and open up to you. Like leads to trust, and trust leads to business.

People only do business with those they know, like, and trust. Knowing someone is often the result of meeting them at an event. Trust comes through liking someone enough to hold a meaningful conversation with them both during and after the event. But *liking* starts with one thing: your smile. Wear it well.

WAY 7

Eat Last

As mentioned briefly in "Way 5," food is almost always a part of networking events. Event organizers know if they offer free food, especially at an event taking place close to dinner time, more people are likely to show up. Food brings people together.

Think back to a recent event you attended where food was served. Where did people tend to congregate? Around the food tables and at the bar, right? Our lives revolve around food. When we want to get to know someone, we invite them to dinner. Food does more than keep guests from going hungry; it gives us a common ground on which to start conversations.

Many simple conversations I have had about the cheese spread or chocolate-covered strawberries (side note: if you want your event to be a huge success, include chocolate-covered strawberries!) led to ongoing friendships and profitable business relationships.

There is one strategy I have used with food that has proven to give me more qualified leads and contacts, and that is to eat last. Usually everyone swarms the food tables first thing. While they are stuffing their mouths with cheese, crackers, and chicken-veggie shish-ka-bobs, I am talking to them. Since they are focused on eating, they are also unable to speak, so they take that opportunity to listen. Of course, I take that opportunity to talk! My bling-y nametag usually opens the door to conversation (see "Way 11") and invokes questions, which I then can take the time to answer.

Eating after everyone else is mostly done forces me to become the listener (see "Way 2"), because I get my plate when everyone else starts talking. This is also a good method to training yourself to listen. Bonus: You have already gotten your talking out of the way!

The only downfall to eating last is that much of the food may be gone before you've had a chance to eat. Or, if the event planning team is very efficient, the leftovers may be whisked away when the eating activity dies down. One way to ensure you get your fill is to go ahead and fix your plate, just wait to eat until others have slowed down. See "Way 9" for another method to handle hunger cravings at events.

WAY 8

Come Early

Most networking events begin at a set time, but most people show up anywhere from fifteen to thirty minutes late. In my opinion, lateness is inconsiderate to the host and crew who worked so hard to organize the event. One way you can thank the host for holding the event (especially if it is free) is to show up early. Get there five or ten minutes early and you will reap some great benefits.

Benefit #1

You have a chance to speak with the host before everyone else arrives and after they've pretty much relaxed from the stress of setup. This lull gives you the opportunity to get to know them better and build a rapport with them. This can lead to major introductions to their contacts later. It may also open the door to invitations to speak at future events because they recognize that you are serious about the group and about your business. Speaking engagements can lead to massive exposure for your business—the type of exposure you will not get from one-on-one conversations. Arriving early also gives you the chance to help the host tidy up loose ends, which makes you a valuable asset to them.

Benefit #2

You are the first person others see when they arrive. If you are the first person at an event, who will new arrivals speak to when they walk in the door? YOU! And the whole point of going to networking events is to get to meet new people and introduce your business to them, right? When yours is one of the only faces in the room, you will naturally be the person people will come up and talk to. Make sure to smile when you greet them (see "Way 6") and remember to *listen* (see "Way 2").

Benefit #3

You will be taken more seriously by your peers who have yet to arrive. If you are a woman in business, being taken seriously is a constant battle. The business world still belongs primarily to men, and unfortunately many businesswomen take the wrong approach to marketing and further weaken our position. I could write an entire book on this subject, but believe me when I tell you if you are a woman and you show up early to a networking event and are dressed professionally (see "Way 16"), you will be noticed!

I'm sure there are more benefits to arriving early than the few I have listed here. Try arriving early to your next event and see what results you get.

WAY 9

Eat Before You Go

Even though many networking events include finger food or sometimes enough food to be a meal, if you wait to eat last (see "Way 7") you run the risk of the organizer clearing away the food before you get a chance to grab a bite. You also may get so caught up in conversations with new people that you forget to eat at all. And if you are like me, you may have food allergies that prevent you from eating at an event.

In order to stay focused on your conversations, you need to have a full stomach and not be sidetracked by the grumbling in your gut. I recommend you eat a hearty snack (or even a full meal) before showing up to any event. I cannot tell you how many times I have left a networking event starving and realized that during the last thirty minutes I was so sidetracked by my stomach, I did not make any good connections with people. To make matters worse, my hunger pains led me directly to a fast-food drive thru for a late-night, fat-filled dinner.

In contrast, think back on times you spoke with someone who was so engrossed in eating their meal that they did not seem to pay any attention to you. How did that make you feel? Remember the reason for the event. Is it to eat a meal? Or is it to meet new prospects, business partners, and vendors? This does not mean you should not eat at all during the event. But it does mean your focus needs to be on your primary reason for attending, not just on the food.

WAY 10

Don't Drink at the Event

Some networking events could be better classified as "drink fests." I'm sure you've been to at least one event that wasn't about networking at all, but instead was a typical after-hours event comprised of people who just wanted to wind down and party. There may be a time and place for such events, but I quickly learned these were not the ideal places for networking. Although most of these events are promoted as *business* networking events, the common conversation is a rant about work, and the common goal seems to be getting drunk. Most after-hours events I've attended were full of corporate employees who are not in my target audience, anyway. For me, these events are a huge waste of time.

Regardless of the type of event, take this never-fail piece of advice to heart: Do not imbibe at business events. There is nothing like getting drunk and making a fool of yourself in front of a crowd to not only ruin your reputation, but turn off those who may have wanted to work with you. When talking to other business owners, the overwhelming majority told me they hate attending events that serve unlimited alcohol because people behave unprofessionally.

I have found that when people do not drink at events, their judgment is clearer. Oftentimes you are able to discern if a prospect is a good one at the first meeting. If your judgment is unclear, you may wind up with a client you do not want, a partnership that quickly goes down-hill, or worse.

You may feel one or two drinks is OK, and honestly, that is totally up to you. But, if you are balancing a planner, briefcase, purse, notebook, plate full of food, and a glass of wine in your hands, how are you ever going to be able to shake hands with someone or not appear clumsy as you shove your face full of food and drink? That image does not give me a good first impression. I would much rather start a conversation with someone who looks alert, interested in me and my business, stands erect, and isn't juggling an armful of objects.

Networking events are all about making a great first impression. If the first impression you give others is as a klutz who is more interested in your wine than the other person, why do you think they would want to do business with you in the future? Save your drinks for the cocktail party. Be the one who stands out and is remembered as a professional.

WAY 11

Wear a Nametag

Most live events or conferences include a nice lanyard and nametag with your name, business name, and the event's logo on it. Most networking events provide sticky nametags and markers for you to use to hastily scrawl your name. (Why is it that that sticky nametags never stick?) I recently invested in a nice, professionally made magnetic nametag (which saves my clothing from puncture wounds), and I have already noticed a difference in how I am perceived.

A nice nametag is just another piece of your professional image. I chose a "bling" tag because the sparkling Swarovski crystals match my fun-loving, creative personality (visit tengrave.

com to see who created mine). Your personality may be more sophisticated or chic. If that's the case, you may prefer a nice burnished metal tag with your logo and name boldly printed on it. Whatever your style, invest in a professional nametag. Here are a few things to consider for your nametag:

Include your logo

Your logo is your brand-at-a-glance. It is an instantly recognizable image that will forever be associated with you and your company. If you do not have a logo, visit ArtsImagine.com and let us create one for you (shameless plug).

Use a block font

If someone has to get inches from your chest to decipher your name or company name on your nametag, you would be better off with the sticky nametag and scrawled handwriting. Take the guesswork out of who you are. Make sure your name is clear, legible, and in easy-to-read block letters.

Add your tag line

If there is room and your tag line is short, add it. Your tag line is a mini-explanation of what you do and is an extension of your brand. My tag line is something that makes people remember me, and is also my one-second "commercial" (see "Way 13"): *I will suck that book out of your head and get it into print!* If your tag line is longer than that, either put a shorter version on your nametag or leave it off.

Include your website

This is another thing to include *only* if there is room. Your website should be on everything, from your business cards and letterhead to the side of your car. It should be the primary resource for people to check out you and your business, and the more you promote it, the better.

You do not want your nametag to be half the size of your chest, so the last two things in this list are optional. At bare minimum, make sure your logo and name are present. After all, the purpose of a nametag is so people may easily learn your *name*.

WAY 12

Bring Your Calendar

When you are in a deep conversation with someone and you really seem to hit it off, you may want to follow up with them later in a more private setting. Unfortunately, more often than not you get home from the event, life gets in the way, and that private meeting never gets scheduled.

I cannot tell you how much potential business I missed out on in my early networking days by not having a way for someone to schedule a meeting with me on the spot. Even when I would follow up later, "life" would get in their way and nailing down that meeting time was nearly impossible. By carrying your planner to the event, you can immediately schedule one-on-one meetings. You'll leave with new appointments on your books and new prospects excited about their private meetings with you.

Another scheduling method I have used since early 2010 is TimeTrade.com. TimeTrade offers an easy online calendar that allows people to schedule appointments with you. It syncs to Google Calendar so you can block out any times you don't want to have a meeting scheduled. You can set up as many calendars as you need for various types of consulting, coaching, general meetings, etc. I have calendars for free consultations, consultations as part of a paid program, special promotional coaching sessions, training sessions for "I am Published!" graduates, and more. This system automatically reminds the other person of their scheduled appointment with you and provides the meeting location or conference call instructions.

I cannot stress enough to you the importance of making it easy for others to meet with you. By using both your planner and an online calendar system like TimeTrade.com, you offer a method of scheduling that is comfortable to your potential prospect and easy for you. As a result, you will see an increase in meetings and business.

WAY 13

Know Your 30-Second (or one-sentence) Commercial

If you have been in business for any length of time, you have probably heard someone mention the concept of the "elevator speech" or "thirty-second commercial." The thirty-second commercial is simply a way for you to quickly express what you do, how you can help someone, and where they can get more information about you. This information is pretty basic, but the way you present it can help you quickly engage people. It's your choice: You can use the interesting method or the boring method to create your short commercial.

The boring method

This method starts with your name. It transitions into your job description, then launches into 500 reasons why your product or service is the best for someone and why they would be stupid not to do business with you. Unfortunately, those representing MLM companies tend to use this method and turn their thirty-second commercial into a fifteen-minute infomercial. This will turn off most prospects and ruin your chances of sharing your business opportunity, product, or services.

The boring method example: "Hello, my name is Kristen Eckstein and I am a book coach. I can help you write and publish your book. People want to work with me because everyone wants to write a book and I know how to help you write it. If you don't already have a book, you need one because it will build credibility for you in your business. You can learn more about me at www.UltimateBookCoach.com."

There are several things wrong with this method. First and most obvious, it is b-o-r-i-n-g!

Second, believe it or not, no one cares about who I am. They would rather know how I can help them. Second, I should be wearing a nametag (see "Way 11"), so they probably already know my name. Third, most people's attention spans time out when they hear "Hello, my name is…" especially if I am not the first introduction they have heard that day. Fourth, I made a claim that "everyone wants to write a book" which is not true. Statistics state that 80 percent of people want to write a book. Assuming everyone wants what I have to offer may make me appear arrogant. About the only thing I did right in the boring method was give my website address at the end.

The interesting method

This method begins with a statement, fact, or question. This attention-grabbing comment draws the listener into everything else that follows. After the question or statement include a short explanation of what you do, how you help people, and how they can contact you for more information.

The interesting method example: "Have you ever thought about writing a book? Wow, you are among the 80 percent of people who want to write one, of which only 20 percent actually do. That's why I do what I do today to help that percentage grow. I can suck that book out of your head and get it into print! I'm Kristen Eckstein, and you can get a ton of free resources to get your book done at www.UltimateBookCoach.com."

Isn't that method much better? Did I grab your attention with that question and statistic, and how I could help you make that sad statistic rise? How would you like to be in that 20 percent who actually writes their dream book? And my tag line is in there, too: *I can suck that book out of your head and get it into print!* It shows I am excited about what I do. I chose a word that invokes a feeling and curiosity to learn more about how this "sucking" occurs, and I offered them "a ton of free resources" to reach a desired result—a finished book. All in less than thirty seconds.

Now, until you become very comfortable and confident in what you provide others, the boring method will work fine for letting people know what you do. It is easier to use that method, and any concise pitch is better than a rambling unclear statement that leaves the listener confused. But if you want to keep people's attention beyond "Hello, my name is…," craft an interesting, creative commercial. You will find that your commercial changes depending on who you are speaking to, but if you know your industry well, you will be confident regardless of the form it takes.

The one-sentence commercial

Here is a secret: the one-sentence commercial can be as simple as your tag line. It should answer the question, "What do you do?" and it should not be a lengthy sentence full of connecting phrases. My one-second commercial is pulled directly from my interesting method example above, "I suck books out of people's heads and get them into print." It quickly answers what I do, yet leaves enough hidden to make people curious and get them asking for more information. If you are a graphic designer, your one-second commercial may be, "I can make you the Pepsi of your industry," or something else that takes a widely recognized brand and shows how you can make your prospect's image that successful in their own field. If you sell supplements, you might say, "I give you the ability to run your business without worrying about sick days."

It is good to have a one-sentence commercial to answer that quick question of, "What do you do?" and a longer thirty-second commercial that explains what you do, who you are, how you can help someone, and where they can get more information about you. If you are entering the speaking market, your thirty-second commercial can be expanded to a thirty- or sixty-minute "Signature Speech," such as what my friend Felicia Slattery teaches at SignatureSpeechSecrets.com. Start with your thirty-second commercial, work it down to that most powerful sentence, then work on expanding it to a longer conversational "speech." Next time someone at a networking event asks what you do, you will be able to blow them away with your confidence!

WAY 14

Research Your Prospects

Most networking events utilize some form of social media to extend invitations, such as Facebook Events, LinkedIn Events, Meetup.com, or Eventbrite. When you are invited to an event that is advertised this way, you can usually see who else is attending. Knowing in advance who else will be there allows you to determine whether it is worth your time to attend, and it gives you a chance to research those who may be good prospects for your business. Here are some steps to take to research your prospects:

Step #1

Know what makes a good prospect. Clearly define your target market. An easy way to do this is to think about your favorite customer. What were they like? Why did you enjoy working for them? What demographic(s) are they in? Write these things down on a short intake form to use when researching prospects to see if they are someone you need to get to know—or may want to skip.

Step #2

In the social media event invite, click on each attendee's name to view his or her profile. If their profiles are private, do a quick Google search for their names to find out what they do. Learn enough about them to fill out your intake form from Step #1 and see if it is worth researching that prospect further. It may be obvious in a matter of seconds that someone is outside your target market—that's good! It should take less than two minutes per person to decide whether you should proceed with them to the next step.

Step #3

Once you have your "I need to meet these people at this event" prospect sheets (intake forms), choose your top three and dig into them a little deeper. If it is a few days before the event, become friends with them on Facebook so you can extensively view their profiles, their likes, and dislikes. Get to know them on a *personal* level before you ever meet them in person.

Note: When requesting friendship on Facebook, be sure to let them know why you are asking. You might even write something like, "I see we're both attending XYZ event next week and I'd like to get to know you more before then." Do not assume everyone wants to be your friend, because the fact is, more people are cracking down on who they connect to on social media and may not accept your request, especially if they have not met you in person yet.

Step #4

Now that you are armed with information about your top three people, you should be able to recognize them when they enter that networking meeting room. Now is not the time to be shy—be bold! Walk right up to them, introduce yourself, and comment about something they like, dislike, or a recent achievement you saw they had in their business. This does a couple things: It impresses them that you took the time to "check them out," and it makes them instantly take you seriously. After all, you have done your homework. Remember to ask them questions—let them talk. By listening (see "Way 2"), you will further impress them. When they ask what it is you do, keep your response short and sweet. Open the door to more questions about your business, but do not hog the spotlight. By keeping the spotlight on them, they will remember you.

Researching your prospects is also a good thing to do before every meeting, even one-on-one consultations. I personally visit the Facebook profiles and websites of those I am meeting either for a phone consultation or in person the week of our meeting. I then use Facebook to stay in touch with them after our meeting. The following short story explains why researching your future connections is so important:

Recently, a prospect requested a meeting with me to talk about his book. We scheduled it three months in advance to fit his schedule. I thought for sure he knew what it is that I do (namely that

I would be helping him get his book "sucked" out of his head and into print) since he was the one who requested the meeting. After he changed our meeting time twice, he then canceled at the last minute—when I was only ten minutes away from our meeting place.

He went on to tell me he had no idea who I was, what I did, and said he would "pass on my services." This showed me he did not feel I was worth the time to research before we met in person, and that I was unimportant to him. (I had extensively researched him as a prospect before our meeting.)

This example shows you how important it is to research your prospects and even potential vendors. If you are thinking of hiring someone to do work for you, it pays to know what they do—before showing up to a meeting! In hindsight, I realize this is not the type of person I want to work with, and the learning experience has helped me put other systems in place to protect my time as well.

When you know who your prospects, customers, and vendors, are and know exactly how you can help them, your confidence will shine.

When you approach others full of confidence (not full of ego or arrogance), you show them you can fulfill a specific need, want, or desire they either currently have or will know they have after speaking with you. So go on, be confident, research your prospects, and make some valuable connections at your next event!

WAY 15

Write Down Your Promises

When my business moved from Ohio to North Carolina, the first thing I did was find every local networking event I could possibly attend, which meant I was going to about three to four each week and meeting hundreds of new people. When you get out in your community and become a powerful networker, you cannot possibly expect yourself to remember everyone you met or the details of every conversation.

I invest in live events for my own continuing education and constantly learn from others at local networking events. As a result, I have a lot of resources stored in my brain that I enjoy sharing with others. At almost every event I attend,

I promise to send someone a document, PDF, website, or some other resource, and if I do not write it down, I inevitably forget to do it. Because of this forgetful nature, I learned early on to carry a small notebook with me to every event. And a pen—do not forget the pen.

Now when I meet someone and discuss sending them a resource, I ask for their business card and write on the back what I am going to do for them—whether that is sending them a resource or simply following up with them for a one-on-one meeting later. If their business cards are glossy (like mine are), I jot down their info in my handy notebook along with a note of what I am to send to them.

The most important thing to remember when promising to send someone you meet anything is to actually send it to them. When you first decide to attend an event, block out time in your schedule either that evening or first thing the next morning to follow up with your prospects and send any resources you promised. Follow up is a discipline, and it is not always easy, especially when you wait until the next morning and your email inbox is full of to-do's that fill up your entire day. However, follow up is critical, so make it a priority.

WAY 16

Dress Professionally

I will admit, it has taken me years to fully understand the importance of dressing professionally. As an artist (albeit a graphic artist), I used to show up to networking events in jeans and a somewhat nice T-shirt. Not exactly the look of a consultant. However, I quickly learned that those clothes made me look younger than I already do, and no one took me seriously. I was asked (more than once) when I would be graduating high school—and I had been out of college for more than five years! Thankfully, I've come a long way in developing my personal, professional style. Here are a few tips to find your perfect look:

Know your style

I have learned that my style is always comfortable, classic yet trendy, and never ever, ever, ever high heels. I have colleagues who wear nothing but high heels and dramatic sophisticated suits in bright reds or black. Once you know your style—what makes you comfortable and yet still professional-looking—take yourself shopping!

Know your brand

It is great to mix up the colors in your wardrobe, but if you really want to get noticed, dress in the colors of your brand (or logo). One of my clients and now a dear friend, "Simply" Sue (SimplySueSpeaks.com), is well known for her teal and lime green brand. Everything she wears falls into those colors. Her logo is a caricature of herself wearing those colors, and even her car is a green that fits her brand! Taking my cue from "Simply" Sue, I began dressing in only the colors of my business's logo: green and blue. This turned out to be quite easy, because most of my wardrobe was already green and blue. However, I did need to purchase a couple of suits and now I can mix and match shirts with those colors in them. I always look classy, yet fun, and everything I wear matches my nametag (see "Way 11"). Though I will branch out and wear other colors, especially when I am speaking, I am easily recognized by the first thing people see when they spot me in a crowd—the colors of my brand.

Know your budget

When you start investing in a professional look, it's easy to break the bank. My secret to dressing well on a budget is to keep a close eye on the consignment and thrift stores, and also to watch the sales at stores that sell professional-style clothing like Kohl's and higher-end stores like the White House-Black Market and Ann Taylor Loft. Check out the outlet stores and stick to the clearance racks. For more tips on finding amazing deals on clothing (and just about everything else), check out my book *Financial Survival: Practical Ways to Save Money*.

Once you start dressing professionally in a style that fits you, your field, and your budget, you will find yourself being taken more seriously by potential prospects and business partners. Your business will grow and you will feel more confident in yourself. So go check out that clearance rack, get a professional look, and I will see you taking care of business at your next event!

WAY 17

Brush Your Teeth

This topic might get a little gross, but it can't be overlooked. I have been to all sorts networking events and have met all sorts of people. Some clearly do not take care of themselves, as in, they don't brush their teeth or wear deodorant. If you are going to represent a company (your company) as one with which other people should spend their hard-earned money, you need to take care of your personal hygiene! This means right before the event, do not just focus completely on the makeup or the right pair of shoes, or making sure you are wearing the perfect tie. Take a quick minute to make sure you smell presentable. Brush your teeth.

Networking events usually get very noisy. In order to hear each other talk, you may have to invade someone else's personal space. Inevitably, you will be breathing on the other person (another reason to avoid that garlic chicken shish-ka-bob they are serving—see "Way 7") and if your breath stinks, that other person will be looking for any reason to exit the conversation. You don't want to bowl people over with bad breath. To the contrary, you want to engage them in conversation so you can connect with them, especially if they are one of your top three prospects (see "Way 14").

In addition to being noisy, these events can get hot as well. When you cram 100 bodies into a small room, people are bound to sweat. Dress in layers and wear deodorant. Whatever you do, do not wear perfume or cologne. Nothing is worse than stuffy air filled with multiple, competing fragrances. And many people are allergic to strong scents, so be considerate of others. Overall, put yourself in the other person's shoes. How would you like to smell the other person's bad breath or body odor? Not a pleasant prospect, is it. So, make sure you are the clean, well-put-together professional.

WAY 18

Follow Up

You may have heard it said before, but it can never be said enough, "Your fortune is in your follow up." When you meet new people at events, be sure to follow up with them right away. Do not let more than a week lapse before you contact them in one way or another.

Following up does not mean adding that person to your email list. Believe it or not, if you exchange business cards with someone, that does not give you the legal right to add them to your e-newsletter. You must get their permission verbally or in writing to use the contact information they share with you. The best sort of follow up is a personal email or social media connection, or both. Automatically adding someone to your email list is against the CAN-SPAM Act of 2003, which is Federal law, and you can be reported and reap dire consequences if you engage in this unethical practice. It also makes people mad, especially busy people who value their time and their contact information.

Here are the exact steps I take to follow up with people after an event:

Step #1

Add the person as your Facebook "Friend." Facebook is where it is happening right now. It is where business is being done—successfully—and where life-changing relationships are being formed. My three best friends in the world I have only met in person once or twice, because we primarily use Facebook to stay in touch. We have built a solid relationship and have even done business together as a result. The first thing I do when meeting someone new is look them up on Facebook. Not everyone is on Facebook (gasp!), so I have other steps as well.

Step #2

Find them on Twitter. I search for their names on Twitter and click "Follow" to show them I am interested in what they have to say. This usually takes less than a minute, and not everyone is on Twitter. Read the bio to make sure you have the right person because there are people with duplicate names.

Step #3

Connect with them on LinkedIn. I admit, I do not use LinkedIn very much. My target audience does not typically hang out there, but it is another medium to get the word out about my business, so I try to connect with people there as well. And I have found many people use LinkedIn, but are not on Facebook or Twitter, so it gives us a chance to stay in touch.

Step #4

Add them to my personal rolodex. I keep my rolodex in an Excel spreadsheet. I have multiple worksheets in one document, each labeled for different groups of people. People are classified as "Current Clients," "Vendors," "Networking Contacts," "Media," "Leads," etc. You can create your rolodex in whatever way makes sense to you, but be sure you include all the information on their business cards, plus some notes about where you met them or what you talked about. This will give you a central place to look them up should they contact you again in the future.

Step #5

Send a personal email. This is the step that takes the most time. I have created a template email for people I meet for the first time, but if we talked about something specific, I always reference that and the event we met at in the message. This shows them it is a personal email directly to them, not a spammed blast sent to everyone. Next to a hand-written note, a personal email means the most to potential prospects and partners.

In this email, I thank them for their time at the event, let them know it was nice meeting them, and *only* here do I invite them to get more information about me. I have several free "ethical bribes" to build my email list. For example, I may offer them the chance to learn more about writing a book at WriteMyBookIn3Days.com, how to get published at ArtOfPublishing.com, or to just sign up for my weekly newsletter at my website. When they sign up through one of those websites, they are giving me written permission to add them to my email list. And written permission is better than verbal permission *any* day, as they could easily say they never told me to add them. This complies with the CAN-SPAM Act and keeps my name clear.

If I follow each of these steps with a new networking connection, it takes about three to five minutes per person. Depending on the size of the event and how many business cards I have to process, I will usually plan one to two hours the next day to follow up. Because sometimes I will throw in some extras, like a note on someone's Facebook wall about how great it was to meet them, the time allotment may grow beyond that. Stay focused on your follow up process and you will breeze through it. Make good follow up a habit. It is easy to get distracted and skip the follow up process, but it is extremely important to the success of your business! Eventually you will build a reputation as a powerful networker who cares about relationships more than money, which ultimately will bring you more referrals and bigger profits.

WAY 19

Offer to Help

If you find a networking group you love and you bond well with its leader, offer to help them with the next event. Even if they do not give you recognition during the event (although many times they may), helping shows that you have a serving heart and both the event coordinator and attendees will recognize it. Being willing to serve is one of the best ways to get what you want—more business.

Helping could include anything from setup, to planning the event, to coordinating sponsorships, to cleaning up afterward. Most small networking group hosts cannot afford event planners, so they come early to set up and leave late after cleaning up. These harried hosts welcome and appreciate a helping hand, and the more you serve, the more you will get asked to take on higher responsibilities within the organization.

When I have helped networking event leaders and coordinators, I have been rewarded with far more than recognition or more business. I have gained relationships within my community that in turn helped me down the road. I have friends I can count on, and those relationships have led to speaking engagements in front of large audiences where I can effectively communicate my message to a captive room. Speaking opportunities allow me to reach more people at once than I could if I simply attended the event.

Helping also means I have been able to teach others about everything from writing a book to crafting a good business card. Even if the attendees don't hire me, I enjoying the pleasure of seeing someone who took my advice get results. When people see results, they remember who gave the advice. And who do they think of when they meet someone who may need my services? Me!

WAY 20

Sponsor the Event

I have yet to meet a networking group that would turn down an offer of sponsorship. Sponsorship can mean anything from donating a door prize, which can be a gift card or one of your products or services, to giving money to help with the event's expenses. In exchange for a door prize or money, your logo may be displayed at the event, and you may even be given a table at which to showcase your products and services.

Sponsoring can extend to conferences or business expos as well. Usually these larger events have structured sponsorship packages that you can choose from ranging from one hundred dollars to several thousand dollars. Obviously the higher the package, the more exposure for your business, but you need to determine which package best fits your needs and budget.

I have sponsored events with cash donations, door prizes, and even a barter of services. For my business, I have found the sponsorship that includes a table to showcase my clients' books and information about my business reaps more reward than simply having my logo represented. The only downfall to a table display is you are pretty much limited to staying in that part of the room, so you need to determine what will fulfill your needs and personality the most. And whatever you do, make sure you thoroughly research and attend a few of the group's functions before committing to sponsor its events. You want to be certain your target market will be present; otherwise it will be a waste of your time and money.

("Leads" groups such as BNI, Chamber groups, etc., often hold larger events, such as business expos, for which they solicit sponsorships.)

# WAY 21

Focus on Building Relationships

The number one most important part to becoming a powerful networker is to focus on building relationships. If you look at people and see dollar signs, you will fail miserably at building a network of people who will uplift, encourage, inspire, and support you and your business when the going gets tough. There are many people who go to these events simply to make a sale. These are people who either appear desperate to get you to buy from them, or are the "untouchable" arrogant types who will walk over anyone to get what they want. Either person is to be avoided—especially when talking about what type of networker *you* will become!

Focusing on building relationships means getting to know people on a personal level, which is why it is so important to be involved in social media. Social media is just that, social. Though many, like me, use it for business, it is also a way to get to know people. If you viewed my Facebook profile while I was writing this book, you saw that was on vacation celebrating my tenth wedding anniversary, enjoying a break from the business of everyday life, hanging out at the beach, shooting a few videos for my business, and about to step out the door and go snorkeling. You can learn a lot about someone within the first few days of observing their Facebook wall. By commenting on things they post, you show yourself as a real person who cares, not just someone out to make a quick buck.

Here are just a few ways social medial has helped me build relationships and my business:

A Twitter conversation about snow out West versus the nice sixty-degree weather we were having in North Carolina led to an invitation to be the guest of a speaker at the first Bob the Teacher SIMPLE conference. After attending that conference, I hired Bob the Teacher as my coach, which led to exponential growth in my business. And now, that speaker is a close, personal friend. And it started with a simple comment about *snow* on Twitter.

During a TweetChat, I sold a publishing package to someone I had never met. At the same virtual event, I "met" my Online Business Manager, Cindy Morus, who I got to meet in person almost a year after hiring her. I made $497 and saved a ton of time by hiring Cindy with that one online chat.

A recent comment on a high-profile speaker's Facebook post led to a personal message from her telling me she had recently referred someone to me for my services. Her time is very limited, so it was a big deal that I heard directly from her—and even a bigger deal that she was referring me without ever having worked with me before! I truly believe because I commented on her posts and built a relationship with her, she noticed me and took the initiative to learn what I do. I never "pitched" her anything and I never actually told her I am in the book business. But by taking an interest in her life, she in turn naturally took an interest in mine.

Here is one final example. I have spent a total of about two hours in person with one of my best friends, and only about two days with another very good friend—both at networking events. Before and after the events, I built relationships with them by "stalking" them online—commenting on Facebook posts, replying to their Twitter posts, and ultimately using Skype to video chat with them once we built a solid foundation to our relationship.

Today I can honestly say these two ladies are my best friends, and as a result we support each other in our businesses and personal lives. I have hired both of them and have done work for each of them. We have worked together, played together, laughed together, and even cried together. Meeting them in person at events was great, but that face-to-face time is limited. Building our relationship began with me reaching out to them on a consistent basis. As a result, they noticed me and started learning more about me. By nurturing our online connection, we developed the solid relationship we share today. Now I feel confident going to them whenever I need anything, and all three of us have found strong support for our businesses we would not have had if I had not taken that initiative to build a solid relationship.

I hope these examples show you the power not only of social media, but of using social media and live events to build relationships that can make a huge impact on your bottom line. If you would like to learn more strategies of how to build these powerful relationships, check out the book *Connect, Communicate & Profit!* by D'vorah Lansky, one of my clients. The information in her book will help you become a master communicator and you will see a direct result in your business profits!

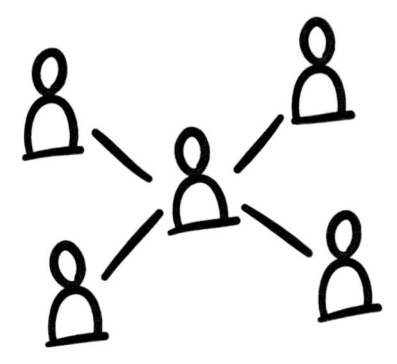

Conclusion

I hope the practical steps outlined in this book will be easy and natural for you to take—and that your business will grow exponentially as a result. Remember, building relationships through networking takes *time*, but the rewards are too numerous to count.

Now that you are armed with this information, go powerfully network your business!

Resources

Get a professional logo design:
ArtsImagine.com

Get a unique marketing tool:
UniqueMarketingTools.com

Get your book written fast:
WriteMyBookIn3Days.com

Nametags with "bling":
TEngrave.com

Online Calendar System:
TimeTrade.com

"Tons of free resources" to write
& publish your book:
UltimateBookCoach.com

Create your Signature Speech™:
SignatureSpeechSecrets.com

Study "Simply" Sue's Branding:
SimplySueSpeaks.com

Get the book *Financial Survival:
Practical Ways to Save Money*
on Amazon.com

Connect on Facebook:
Facebook.com/WritingFan

Connect on Twitter:
Twitter.com/imaginestudios

Connect on LinkedIn:
LinkedIn.com/in/imaginestudios

Free publishing workshop:
ArtOfPublishing.com

Bob the Teacher's SIMPLE Event
KristenRecommends.com/simple

TweetChat your next event!
TweetChat.com

Connect, Communicate & Profit!
by D'vorah Lansky:
ConnectCommunicateAndProfit.com

About the Author

Kristen's clients call her "The Ultimate Book Coach." She started writing when she was five years old and read her first "adult" level novel when she was nine.

In 2003, Kristen served as the marketing director for a vanity publishing company that featured a traditional publishing arm. That year she published her first two books.

When she left that company, she and her husband co-founded Imagine! Studios, LLC, an art and media production company. They soon began publishing authors' books again under their own label, and she published a third book of her own. A relocation in 2006 caused them to hand that portion of their business off to another capable publisher, and she began her present role as a publishing consultant.

In 2009, she wrote her fourth book in three and a half days, and in early 2011, she wrote and published the first two books in the *21 Ways*™ series.

Kristen's reputation is to "suck" books out of people's heads and get them into print through "Ghost Publishing," a term she coined to define her exclusive done-for-you Indie publishing program. Through the course of her publishing career, she has helped dozens of authors independently publish. Several of her clients have been traditionally published as a direct result of going through her program.

Her favorite thing in the world is to see YOU hug your book for the very first time!

That is, next to chocolate for breakfast.

You can write a book in 3 1/2 days!

Get **FREE** instant access to my training video and watch and listen as I share my secrets for finishing your book in 3 1/2 days!

> **Rebecca Morus** I just listened to your free training video on "Write Your Book in 3.5 days! I was thrilled with the insightful information you provided. Although, I have not ventured into writing books- I've made many attempts to write scripts. You provided a "real world" instructions on how to actually finish those ideas swarming in my head! I'll definitely be able to use this on my next project!
> 42 minutes ago · Like

> **Bethany Williams** Thank you for sharing this. I took some wonderful tips from this video. And the fact that it is FREE is extremely generous. Sharing any information about writing for FREE is quite a gift. I can't thank you enough! Also, I am inspired to buckle down and focus. A great kick in the pants. Just what I needed today. =)
> 6 hours ago · Unlike · 1 person

WriteMyBookIn3Days.com

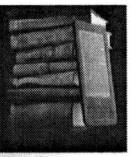

80% of people want to get published…

only 20% of them make it happen.

FREE VIDEO TRAINING

Have you always wanted to publish a book?

You've heard having a book is one of the best ways to boost your credibility, but…

You have no clue how to get your book published or just feel this may be too overwhelming to take on right now in your business?

Learn the ins and outs of the three types of publishing step-by-step!

ArtOfPublishing.com

Don't miss a single book in the series!

Look for more *21 Ways*™ books at:

21WaysBooks.com